Cookin' Up Your Retirement Plan

By
Marcia MacDonald Mantell

Design & Illustrations by
Geralyn Miller

Mantell Retirement Consulting, Inc.

This discussion guidebook is intended for personal use only. It is educational and informational and should not be construed as professional financial advice. Retirement laws are subject to changes. Please consult a tax advisor for the most current rules and regulations.

Marcia MacDonald Mantell ©2022
2nd Edition ©2024

Mantell Retirement Consulting, Inc.
Plymouth, MA

Dedication

To the Baby Boomer generation whose members are fearlessly facing
the uncharted and untamed waters of whatever this
new "retirement" era is going to be.

You are the pioneers who are reimagining, redesigning, and
reinventing the very ideas about retirement.

It's a tough job.

Yet who better to take it on and lead future generations forward?

But first, grab a cup of coffee or tea, sit down at your kitchen table,
and get ready to create some new recipes for your own retirement.

Cheers to the Boomers!

Table of Contents

Take your time.
Don't get mad at the person you are talking to.
Experiment with new ideas about your retirement years.
Enjoy the process.

Welcome to my kitchen, where we'll be discussing lots of important topics that become the basic ingredients to your retirement plan. We'll focus on how you'll spend your time, what you want to do to make your retirement wonderful, and how you can turn your hard-earned savings into a paycheck throughout a long and happy retirement.

A Delicious Lasagna

I look at making this transition to retirement much like making a lasagna. It takes time and some effort to create a big pan of delicious lasagna:

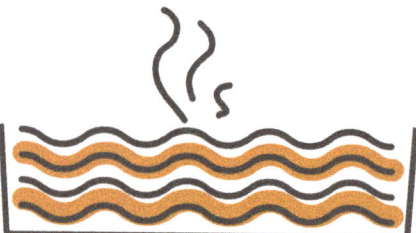

- How long will you slow cook your special sauce?
- Which spices do you use? Fresh basil or dried? Lots of oregano or a little?
- Do you add extras to the ricotta to spice it up a bit?
- Or do you prefer cottage cheese?
- What about the meat? Ground beef, sausage, or pork? Or are veggies your thing?
- Will you cook your noodles first or use the no-cook kind?
- Do you make a bechamel or just go with a variety of cheeses?

There are so many different ingredients each family uses in their "signature dish." So many different options for traditional, vegetarian, gluten-free, or vegan varieties. You get to choose all the ingredients, just like you get to choose how to build your own retirement years. Let's make sure it is delicious!

Make Your Masterpiece.

Common to all lasagnas is that each ingredient is individually delicious. But the magic doesn't happen until you assemble the entire dish, layer by layer. Top it with cheese, and bake until melty, golden brown, and the sauce bubbles around the edges.

Layer by layer is how you'll build your plan for your special, unique, exciting retirement. It will take some time, some experimentation, perhaps a few tries to make retirement work for you. But, after you "bake" your ideas for a while, you too will have a masterpiece.

Let's create your masterpiece for retirement.
Right at your own kitchen table.

How to use this book

Talk with People

Much like making your signature recipe, you can use this discussion guide in many ways. The main idea, however, is to talk about your ideas and plans for retirement with the people you will retire with. It may be your husband or wife, your partner, your grown children, a best friend, cousins, or even your own parents or older relatives who will be a big part of your retirement.

It's when we hear our ideas, our wants and wishes, and the things we don't want to do in retirement out loud, that this obscure thing we call our "retirement years" starts to take some shape.

Create your own recipes for retirement

Here are some tips for creating your own retirement menu. In each chapter you'll find a discussion guide followed by a worksheet. At the end of the book you'll find the signature piece called "Planning Your Retirement Menu: Plan A, B, + C."

It's best to go through each section in order and build parts of your plans along the way.

The discussion guides and worksheets

Each of the 6 sections should help you identify and assemble all your ingredients to build your plans for retirement. As you go through the discussion guides and worksheets in each section:

- Be honest about your view of retirement. Many people love the idea of retiring … and an equal number greatly dislike the very idea.

- Discuss the topics laid out in each discussion guide, answering the variety of questions that may apply to your life and your life in retirement.

- Use the blank spaces to jot down your thoughts, ideas, wishes. And color in the doodle pages as you think about all the possibilities for your retirement years.

- Follow the "Get Cookin'" suggestion at the end of each section to fill out the worksheet that follows.

GET COOKIN'! ▶

- The information you fill out in the worksheets will help you construct your Plan A, B, +C.

Planning Your Retirement Menu with Plan A, B, +C

The final step is to create your own "menu" for retirement. Using Plan A, B, + C at the end of this guidebook allows you to clearly see what you can do with your time. Plus, you'll get a look at how much each year could cost and how much money you'll have to spend in retirement. (This is not a financial plan. It is an overview of the layers you are assembling of your own retirement years.)

Plan A, B, + C allows you to tie together your wishes and wants along with your financial resources to see what may be possible. Think of this as an adventure. You're going to put on your apron and mix a little of this with a little of that to get a taste of your lasagna.

TIME TO SLICE & DICE!

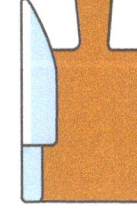

Thinking about my retirement and my future as a "retiree"

Retiree? I'm going to be a retiree? How did that happen so fast?

For many, nearing retirement is a surprise. For others, they've been dreaming of this day for decades. Take a deep breath, grab a box of chocolates, and talk about what being a retiree might be for you. Jot down your thoughts about each of these three starting topics.

In general, I am:
- ► Looking forward to retirement?
- ► Uncertain about the idea of retiring?
- ► Dreading the very thought of it?

My thoughts, views, opinions about retirement.
- ► Where do those thoughts come from?
- ► Will you embrace them or redefine them?
- ► Has my view about retirement changed?
- ► How will my life change when my spouse/partner retires?

Let's talk about my retirement:
- ► Do I want to retire?
- ► When might I want to retire?
- ► How will I know I'm ready to retire?
- ► What will I do when I'm not going to work every day?

Who will depend on me during my retirement years?

▶ Are there family members who you will care for? Friends? Members of your community or church?
▶ What will your role be and for how long?

PERSON	MY ROLE

Where will I live throughout retirement?

Think about your housing and living options in phases. Where will you be in your early years of retirement? What about each subsequent decade as you age? Is your preference to age in place or do you want options in case your health declines? Who will you rely on if you need help?

At Retirement
- Staying in the family home?
- Upsizing or downsizing?
- Tax considerations?

In your 70s
- Condo living?
- Same area or somewhere new?
- "Snowbird"?

In your 80s & beyond
- Where is it easier?
- In with your children?
- Assisted living?

GET COOKIN'! ▶ Spend some time thoughtfully filling out the *"Dream up Your Retirement Menu"* worksheet.

MAKING THE TRANSITION TO RETIREMENT
SECTION 1: WORKSHEET

Dream up Your Retirement Menu

As you think about what your future years of retirement might hold, start with the possibilities. What would you do if money were no object? What would make you happy? Or help you fulfill a long-deferred dream? How will you make the most of this time in your life?

Ask yourself these questions: What would I do during my retirement years if I had the money to do anything? What will be on my retirement menu?

(Select all you might consider)

- ☐ Personal growth – learn a new language, write a book
- ☐ Pursue the arts – music, performing, painting
- ☐ Join a gym, athletic training, take up a sport
- ☐ Give more to my community
- ☐ Spend more time with my family
- ☐ Travel the world and gain new experiences
- ☐ Enjoy more quiet time and less structure
- ☐ Start a new business
- ☐ Teach in my industry or college/school
- ☐ Join a non-profit board
- ☐ Become a consultant
- ☐ Spend more time on my hobbies / crafting
- ☐ Do something in the gig economy – rent rooms in my house, driver, etc.
- ☐ Use my expertise in a new/different way
- ☐ Continue to work, but maybe fewer hours
- ☐ _____
- ☐ _____
- ☐ _____
- ☐ _____

INGREDIENTS THAT GIVE DREAMS THEIR POWER

Ideally, do I want to Upsize? Downsize? Keep size?

- ☐ Build a family compound?
- ☐ Buy a second home in a resort area / remote location / waterfront / mountains?
- ☐ Retreat to a small cottage?
- ☐ Buy a villa in Italy?
- ☐ Live abroad for a year or more?
- ☐ Buy a boat?
- ☐ Help at a winery, farm, brewery, restaurant?
- ☐ Start an art or dance studio?
- ☐ Buy a classic car to restore?
- ☐ _____
- ☐ _____

Section 1 Discussion Guide: Thinking about my retirement and my future as a "retiree" 6

It's all about the prep work

Keeping your dreams in mind, now think about the years you have from now until you retire. What can you do now to prepare to pursue your dreams? What new and different ideas would you like to try before leaving your job? A recipe by itself has no soul. You, the cook, bring soul to the recipe!

What would I like to do before retirement that can help me get ready to make a successful transition into retirement? How can I better prepare for retiring to something, not just retiring from my job?

BRING YOUR SOUL TO THE RECIPE!

- ☐ Sell my current house and relocate to new area
- ☐ Sell my current house and stay in current area
- ☐ Buy a farm / store / restaurant / B&B
- ☐ Renovate current house to enjoy
- ☐ Talk to employer about phased retirement or going part-time
- ☐ Consider an early-retirement package
- ☐ Go back to school for a new degree or complete an education goal
- ☐ Join a new club – women's group, men's club, community group
- ☐ Take a class at a community college or vocational school
- ☐ Volunteer at an organization in my region
- ☐ Read and research options for extended travel
- ☐ Join a campaign for a cause or political candidate
- ☐ _____
- ☐ _____
- ☐ _____

Making retirement the best it can be: books you might find helpful

Read articles on:
Boomer Retirement Briefs

Available at:
BARNES & NOBLE BOOKSELLERS   **amazon**

▶ **Action Step:** Get your own copy of these books and find other recommendations in my blog: BoomerRetirementBriefs.com.

Combine the flavors that you love

What would mean the most to you as you think about all the years you'll have in retirement? What will make your retirement more fulfilling? More exciting? Better?

First, choose your top 5 ideas you'd like to try out in retirement …

TOP 5 INGREDIENTS

1. _____

2. _____

3. _____

4. _____

5. _____

… then create your "menu planner" to see where and when you'll try out some of your top 5 ingredients. Can you experiment and try out some of your ideas before retirement? Or is your schedule too busy now and you'll have to wait until your first years of retirement? For example:

YEAR 1	2023 – 2 years before my expected retirement		
JAN		JULY	
FEB	Find a place in Arizona to try out as a winter get-away – start with 4 weeks	AUG	
MAR		SEPT	
APR		OCT	Sign up for a volunteer role at the art museum – let's see how that goes!
MAY		NOV	
JUNE	Check out the local colleges – any courses I might want to take before retirement?	DEC	

Now, look forward for the next 5 years. What ideas are you going to give a try?
Even one or two ideas each year will help you see into your future.
Fill out your plans on the following pages.

YEAR 1   YEAR _____   # of years before I retire _____

JAN	JULY
FEB	AUG
MAR	SEPT
APR	OCT
MAY	NOV
JUNE	DEC

YEAR 2   YEAR _____   # of years before I retire _____

JAN	JULY
FEB	AUG
MAR	SEPT
APR	OCT
MAY	NOV
JUNE	DEC

YEAR 3   YEAR _____   # of years before I retire _____

JAN	JULY
FEB	AUG
MAR	SEPT
APR	OCT
MAY	NOV
JUNE	DEC

YEAR 4   YEAR _____   # of years before I retire _____

JAN	JULY
FEB	AUG
MAR	SEPT
APR	OCT
MAY	NOV
JUNE	DEC

YEAR 5   YEAR _____   # of years before I retire _____

JAN	JULY
FEB	AUG
MAR	SEPT
APR	OCT
MAY	NOV
JUNE	DEC

MAKING THE TRANSITION TO RETIREMENT
SECTION 2: DISCUSSION GUIDE
Planning "3 squares" a day

Whether you're the chef or the diner, you may be like most people and plan your daily routine around breakfast, lunch, and dinner. When thinking about your retirement years, it might be helpful to plan that same structure for the next 11,000 days. As you envision your life in retirement, you'll also want to consider how you'll keep an active social life and how you'll get out and about. Let's talk about three important retirement realities that are often neglected when planning.

1. Sharing Meals

From kindergarten through working years our lives centered around a place we've taken for granted: the humble cafeteria. The food was not always the highlight, but being in large groups created built-in connections. Think about how you will share meals and lively conversation when there is no cafeteria and no one around to grab for lunch.

☐ How many lunches or dinners will you eat alone each week?

☐ How many days each week will you eat with someone other than your spouse or partner?

☐ Where will your circle of friends meet up for weekly lunches?

☐ Are you building in poker games, book clubs, or knitting classes each week that include snacks and potlucks?

☐ Have you explored craft breweries in your area for meeting new people?

Schedule time in your retirement weekly and monthly routine to bring back the dinner party, go on a picnic, or set up group lunches at your favorite restaurant.

Your ideas for building shared meals into weekly retirement life:

1. _____

2. _____

3. _____

SECTION
DISCUSSION 2

2. Building my social network...not my social media

When you no longer have a built-in network at work, who will you see and talk to every day? When your household routine changes, how will you adapt?

Thinking about life in retirement is monumentally different from your last 40+ years of building a career, taking on various jobs, raising a family, and maintaining a household. Activity was automatically built in. It will take some doing to create an entirely new structure and routine. The time to start building your social network starts now. And it's not on your computer or smartphone!

 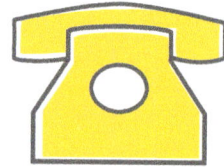 

Facebook vs. the Phone

Establishing and keeping up with your human connections are most important in retirement. And may be hard to achieve with friends and family scattered all over the globe.

☐ How often each week will you have a social, in-person engagement?

☐ How many people will you talk to every day? Who are they?

☐ How long do you spend on Facebook or other social media every day?

☐ Who will be among your trusted friends when the going gets tough?

Schedule time in your retirement daily routine to pick up the phone, use Skype or Facetime, and talk to your friends and family. It's not the same as texting or posting a kitty video.

Your ideas for incorporating human connections into daily retirement life:

1. _____

2. _____

3. _____

3. Getting out and about

As you age, it may become more challenging to get out and about. But it's more important than ever to continue participating in activities and events involving others. Build in extra time to get where you're going and use any devices needed to be safe. Everyone likes to feel needed and important. As we age throughout a long retirement, we'll need to learn to ask others for some help. They will help. In fact, they will most often be more than happy to pick you up for the family parties or get you to an event. It's all in how you ask and how far in advance you can plan. Talk turkey about these kinds of retirement realities:

- ☐ How will you get to the restaurant or birthday party or sports event?

- ☐ Have you traded in high-heels for more practical, yet still stylish, shoes so you can walk further and be more comfortable?

- ☐ Did you buy season tickets and passes to museums, concerts, and events in your area? Great! But how will you get there and back?

- ☐ Are you up-to-date and familiar with the public transportation options in your area? When did you last try them out?

- ☐ Will you be comfortable going out and about if you need to use a cane or other mobility support?

Make sure you get those ride-share apps on your phone and learn how to use them. The convenience can't be beat. And it's cheaper than parking. See if you can take a bus to the airport or train station. And, talk to your local Council on Aging (COA) about the transportation options they offer to get you to doctor's appointments and shopping destinations.

Your ideas for building outside activities into weekly retirement life:

1. _____

2. _____

3. _____

Cookin' with the grandkids

One of the great joys of retirement for many is the possibility of grandchildren. If you expect grandchildren will be part of your retirement, how much involvement would ideally like to have? And how much of your time will your kids and daughters/sons-in-law find helpful as you embrace grandparenthood?

SECTION 2 DISCUSSION

Very Involved

- I'm moving in!
- Have my children and grandchildren move in with me or be right around the corner
- Provide day care or significant amount of weekly support
- Enjoy every minute of these years that I didn't get with my own children

Semi Involved

- Call me often!
- Offer to provide some backup support when needed
- Plan fun outings and special events for my grandchildren
- Have sleepovers and spend holidays together, passing along our family traditions

Occasionally Involved

- Let me think about it.
- My children won't need me to be involved on a frequent basis
- My grandchildren live far away; we'll spend holidays together
- I'll be busy filling my days in retirement, but will enjoy an occasional dinner or weekend with the grandkids

IF I BECOME A GRANDMA, I'LL WANT TO BE: _____

IF I BECOME A GRANDPA, I'LL WANT TO BE: _____

 GET COOKIN'! ▶ Spend some time filling out the *"My Plans for Retirement"* worksheet.

Not sure where to get started?

Check out these websites for ideas, information, and ways to incorporate important connections into your retirement days and weeks.

 **MIT's Age Lab**: https://agelab.mit.edu/

 **AARP**: https://www.aarp.org/
AARP Foundation: https://www.aarp.org/aarp-foundation/

 **National Council on Aging**: https://ncoa.org/
Your local Council on Aging / Center for Active Living: Google your town or county

SECTION 2: WORKSHEET

My Plans for Retirement

How will you spend your time in retirement?

Creating a structure to your days when you no longer work can be one of the more challenging parts of retirement. It may sound fun to have no plans or to sit on the couch all day and watch TV. But after a few weeks of total freedom, boredom can set in.

Take some time to think about all that time off. Thirty years of no commitments, no obligations, nothing to do. That's 10,957 days of freedom. Could be trouble on the horizon!

The ideas you are thinking about or want to explore become key ingredients to your retirement recipe. There are no right or wrong ideas, just the possibility of finding ways you want to spend at least some of your time and how your days may change over time.

Start your planning by trying to answer questions such as:
- What do I want to do with my time?
- How do I want to structure my days?
- How will I make a contribution and be productive?

Stumped? So am I! Try filling out the following sections and see what you come up with:
- Ideas from current retirees
- Family and friend commitments
- A 1-week view of your retirement
- Travel plans
- Volunteering
- Working in retirement
- Pursing hobbies, learning new things, exploring new paths

Who knows – you might like your ideas so much that you'll retire sooner than you thought!

Ideas from current retirees

What are the retirees you know doing in retirement? Have you seen or heard of any ideas that are particularly interesting to you? Make a list of vocations, hobbies, volunteer organizations or jobs that you might be interested in.

Retirees I know ... and what they are doing	Ideas I like	Ideas I don't like

Family & friend commitments

Have you become the "holiday house" for some of the family get-togethers? Are you the one who plans barbeques and reunions with your friends? Do you have elderly relatives you may need to care for in retirement? Will you babysit your grandchildren? Think about the family commitments you could have in retirement and how much time you might spend on them.

Family commitments I may have	Hosting family or friend events	Holiday Fun

Create a 1-week view of your retirement

First, lightly shade in the boxes when you are at work. Then, try filling out what a typical week could look like when you are living in retirement. Having some structure to your week may help you see yourself as a retiree.

SECTION 2 WORKSHEET

	SUN	MON	TUES	WED	THU	FRI	SAT
7-8 AM							
8-9 AM							
9-10 AM							
10-11 AM							
11-12 PM							
12-1 PM							
1-2 PM							
2-3 PM							
3-4 PM							
4-5 PM							
5-6 PM							
6-7 PM							
7-8 PM							
After 8 PM							

© 2024 MRC Inc. For personal use only

Section 2 Worksheet: My Plans for Retirement 18

Travel plans

Many near-retirees think travel will be a big part of their retirement. What are your travel plans and where do you most want to go? Start your list here.

Places to Travel	When to go	How long to stay	Travel partner(s)

Volunteering

There is a tremendous need for volunteers in every community. Are you planning to spend some of your time in retirement giving back in some way? Start a list of possible organizations who could benefit from your time and expertise.

Which organizations could use my help?	What might I do in a volunteering capacity?	How much time am I willing to spend?

Think about organizations you've participated in or are interested in. There are many options including: your local Council on Aging, food pantries, Girl Scouts/Boy Scouts, Big Brother–Big Sister, International exchanges, coaching, local boards, care-giving, United Way, Red Cross, animal shelters, religious organizations, and many more. Search for volunteer activities at www.VolunteerMatch.org or www.IdeaList.org or Engage.PointsofLight.org

Working in Retirement

It's really not a bad idea! Many people spend 30, 40 or more years building an expertise in their field. Why turn it off overnight? Continuing to work in retirement, either full-time or part-time may be just what you want to do. What might your options look like?

Work options	How long do I want to do this job?	What will it take to do this job?
Staying at my job full-time		
Reducing hours from full-time to part-time		
Changing to a new company or new job		
Taking my expertise and becoming a consultant		
Hanging my own shingle		
Starting or buying a business		
Working a gig job (driving, renting rooms, etc.)		
Buying/Managing rental property		
Something else?		

Pursing Hobbies, Learning New Things, Exploring New Paths

Retirement can be a wonderful time to spread your wings and delve into new areas just because you can. What's on your list to learn and explore?

Hobbies	Education	Exploration

Take Some Time to Think

There's no right answer to what you want your retirement to be. It may be a series of starts and restarts. Life might throw in a curve ball. Take some time to doodle and noodle what you might want your one, very special retirement to be. Jot down some thoughts and ideas whenever they pop in your head.

Plan for 10 Essential Ingredients in your Retirement Menu

Retirement may well be one-quarter of your lifetime. It's a different time of life with a big challenge ahead: how to age gracefully. Understanding these 10 "facts of retirement life," or essential ingredients, should help make your planning more focused and purposeful. Talk about all 10 from your perspective.

GOOD INGREDIENTS
MAKE THE DIFFERENCE!

1	**Odds are in your favor to live a long time** • Women who live to 65 have a 50/50 chance of living to 87 • Men who live to 65 have a 50/50 chance of living to 85 • BUT… you need to plan for the odds of living beyond the averages. • Initial planning horizon: Age 95	**Inputs to Your Plans** My Retirement Planning Horizon is to age _____. That means I could spend _____ years in retirement. My spouse's/partner's planning age is _____ and could spend _____ years in retirement.
2	**Dealing with debt and building credit remains important** • Average debt for Boomers is $97,000 (includes mortgages) • Average credit card debt for those aged 55 – 64 is $8,200 • Average FICO credit score for ages 60+ is 749/850 • Ideally, you'll want to pay off all non-mortgage debt before you retire • Some believe paying off the mortgage is also important; others prefer the tax deduction	**Inputs to Your Plans** I/we have _____ years to go on my mortgage. My payoff date is _____. My/our credit card debt is $_____ today. My FICO score is_____. My spouse's/partner's credit card debt is $_____ today. His/Her FICO score is _____
3	**With aging comes aches, pains, illness** • 85% of older adults have at least one chronic health condition • 60% have at least two chronic conditions	**Inputs to Your Plans** How will my health influence my retirement plans? How will my spouse's/partner's health influence our retirement plans?
4	**Ageism is alive and well; you may lose your job earlier than planned** • 66% of full-time workers lose their jobs involuntarily before "retirement" age • Only 10% of displaced workers return to their prior income level	**Inputs to Your Plans** I need a Plan B. And a Plan C. Let's look at the possibility of losing my job earlier than I'm planning. Or if my spouse/partner loses their job earlier than ideal.

SECTION
DISCUSSION
3

5	**Living alone requires active preparation**
	• In the 65+ age group:
	  - 45% of women are married;
	   55% live alone
	  - 70% of men are married;
	   30% live alone
		Inputs to Your Plans
		How am I/we building community, network, support systems today to prepare for living alone at some point in retirement?

6	**There's no such thing as "affordable" health care** • Medicare + Medigap for a person in excellent health est. = $6,000/yr • Medicare + Medigap for a person in poor health est. = $14,000/yr • Prescription drug costs are additional	**Inputs to Your Plans** Use Medicare.gov estimate your personal costs See Section 4 for a detailed budget worksheet to estimate your health care costs
7	**Investing philosophies need to adjust to deliver both income and growth** • For money to last 30+ years, target a 3% to 5% initial withdrawal rate • On average, there is a recession every 4 – 5 years • Remaining in the equity market is a key investing strategy throughout retirement	**Inputs to Your Plans** How much I can pull from my investment accounts at a 3% or 4% withdrawal rate. $_____ Pull all my accounts together and prepare to meet with a retirement income advisor on (date)_____
8	**Inflation will eat away your hard-earned savings & drive costs up over time** • At 2.5% inflation, purchasing power is cut in half in about 25 years • At 4% inflation, purchasing power is cut in half in about 18 years	**Inputs to Your Plans** How much could groceries cost in 10 years? _____ In 25 years? _____ Do I have a plan to increase my income to address inflation? Yes / No
9	**Taxes are often one of the top 2 or 3 highest expenses in retirement** • You'll owe income tax on most retirement plans, Traditional IRAs, pensions, Social Security, etc. • Property taxes, excise taxes, state taxes continue every year	**Inputs to Your Plans** Do I have a tax professional on my team? _____ Review the IRS Tax Guide for the Retiree (IRS Pub. 4190) for tips about filing taxes once you reach age 65
10	**Your estate and legacy plans matter – and need to be well-documented** • Estate plans are formal, legal documents including health care directives and instructions for passing your assets to beneficiaries • Legacy plans are more informal written instructions for the values and valuables you want to leave to selected individuals	**Inputs to Your Plans** I will update my estate plan by: _____ I have inventoried my items to pass along: Yes / No I have detailed instructions for my digital assets: Yes / No See section 6 for more details

LONGEVITY is the game-changer in modern American retirement planning.

Women and men need to plan to live for a long time.

LIVE TO 65 > Plan beyond 87

LIVE TO 75 > Plan beyond 89

LIVE TO 85 > Plan beyond 93

LIVE TO 65 – Plan beyond 85

LIVE TO 75 – Plan beyond 87

LIVE TO 85 – Plan beyond 92

When planning your retirement, plan for the possibility
you'll live well beyond these averages.

Unless you have a known health issue, plan to at least age 95.
Plan for longer if your parents are already nearing 100.

GET COOKIN'! ▶

Spend some time thoughtfully filling out the
**"Mark your retirement planning milestones
and key birthdays" worksheet.**

Then enter your key dates in Plan A, B, +C
in the "milestones" boxes.

MAKING THE TRANSITION TO RETIREMENT
SECTION 3: WORKSHEET

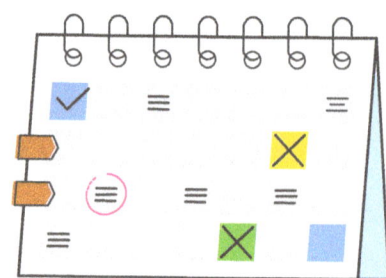

Mark Your Retirement Planning Milestones and Key Birthdays

Pencil in these important ages and dates. They become key anchor points when planning your retirement menu. You'll also enter them in your Plan A, B, +C planner.

Whether you are planning to retire or not, there are many important retirement-related dates you need to know about and deadlines to lock in your calendar. You won't want to be the one who misses key dates and then is frustrated at the consequences and financial penalties.

Just like planning for anniversaries, family reunions or milestone birthdays, it's a good idea to mark these dates on your behalf and for your spouse or partner. Write in your specific dates that correspond to ages listed below and read why these ages/dates are so important.

AGE 50

Build your initial Retirement Income Plan: Formalize a written plan for how you will create your "paycheck" in retirement.

Save more: Catch up contributions are now available in your employer plans and IRAs.

The year I turn 50: _____

The year my spouse/partner turns 50: _____

Notes: _____

_____

_____

AGE 55

Revise your Retirement Income Plan: Review your plan and determine what changes should be applied to update it.

Deal with Debt: Set up a plan for paying down as much debt as possible before you retire.

The year I turn 55: _____

The year my spouse/partner turns 55: _____

Notes: _____

_____

_____

AGE 59½

Penalty free distributions: IRAs can now be tapped without a 10% early withdrawal penalty.

CAUTION! Remember that IRAs are intended for your retirement. Just because the penalty goes away doesn't mean you should dip into your IRAs yet.

The year I turn 59½: _____

The year my spouse/partner turns 59½: _____

Notes: _____

_____

_____

AGE 60

Update your Retirement Income Plan: It's time to fine tune your plan with specific, detailed numbers. Map out a new Plan A, B, and C.

Look ahead: When might you realistically retire? What will you do with your time? What are your plans for Social Security? How will you pay for health care in retirement?

The year I turn 60:_____

The year my spouse/partner turns 60: _____

Notes: _____

_____

_____

_____

AGE 62

Early Access to Social Security: This is the earliest age to claim your Social Security retirement benefits.

CAUTION! You'll lock in a permanent reduction of up to 30% of your monthly income. That's a lot of cash out of your "paycheck" in your 80s and 90s.

The year I turn 62:_____

The year my spouse/partner turns 62: _____

Notes: _____

_____

_____

_____

AGE 65

Eligible for Medicare: This universal health insurance program becomes available the first day of the month you reach age 65. When your coverage starts depends when you enroll.

CAUTION! If you have a younger spouse, there may be a coverage gap. If you are enrolling in Medicare, what will your spouse have for coverage?

The year I turn 65:_____

The year my spouse/partner turns 65: _____

Notes: _____

_____

_____

_____

_____

AGE 66-67

Full Retirement Age (FRA): If your birthday is in 1946 through 1959 FRA is 66, or 66 and some number of months. If you were born in 1960 or later, your FRA is 67. This is when your full, unreduced Social Security retirement benefit is available to you.

CAUTION! Your FRA is an exact month and year. Know the exact date when your full benefit becomes available before filing your claim.

The year I reach FRA: _____

The year my spouse/partner reaches FRA:_____

Notes: _____

_____

_____

_____

_____

AGE 70

Last Date: This is the oldest age to earn Social Security "delayed retirement credits" – an 8% per year bonus for waiting to claim.

CAUTION! After age 70, there is no reason to delay claiming. You'll leave money on the table.

The year I turn 70:_____

The year my spouse/partner turns 70: _____

Notes: _____

_____

_____

AGE 71

Last Chance: Convert tax-deferred retirement assets to a Roth IRA before taking Required Minimum Distributions, if that is part of your plan.

CAUTION! Take note if converting will increase your Medicare Part B premiums.

Good Idea: Required Minimum Distributions are easier to manage if your accounts are consolidated and well-organized. Take the time now to get organized and update beneficiary designations.

The year I turn 71:_____

The year my spouse/partner turns 71: _____

Notes: _____

_____

_____

_____

_____

_____

_____

AGE 72 or 73 or 75

Required Minimum Distributions (RMD) Begin: The IRS requires you to begin taking a portion of your retirement savings as taxable income. You must take money from all Traditional IRAs, 401(k)s, 403(b)s, and other tax-deferred retirement accounts every year beginning at 72 or 73 or 75, depending on your birthday.

CAUTION! Failure to take a RMD may result in a 25% penalty payable to Uncle Sam!

Good Idea: You can make qualified charitable distributions directly from your IRA to meet RMD and save on taxes (beginning as early as age 70 1/2).

The year I turn 72 or 73 or 75: _____

The year my spouse/partner turns 72 or 73 or 75:

_____

Notes: _____

_____

_____

_____

_____

See page 47 for more information

SIMPLY SAID, IT'S TIME TO LOCK IN KEY DATES AND MILESTONES ON YOUR RETIREMENT MENU.

"You are never too old to set a new goal or dream a new dream."

– C.S. Lewis

How much will I spend each year in retirement?

The further you are from retirement, the less precise you can be

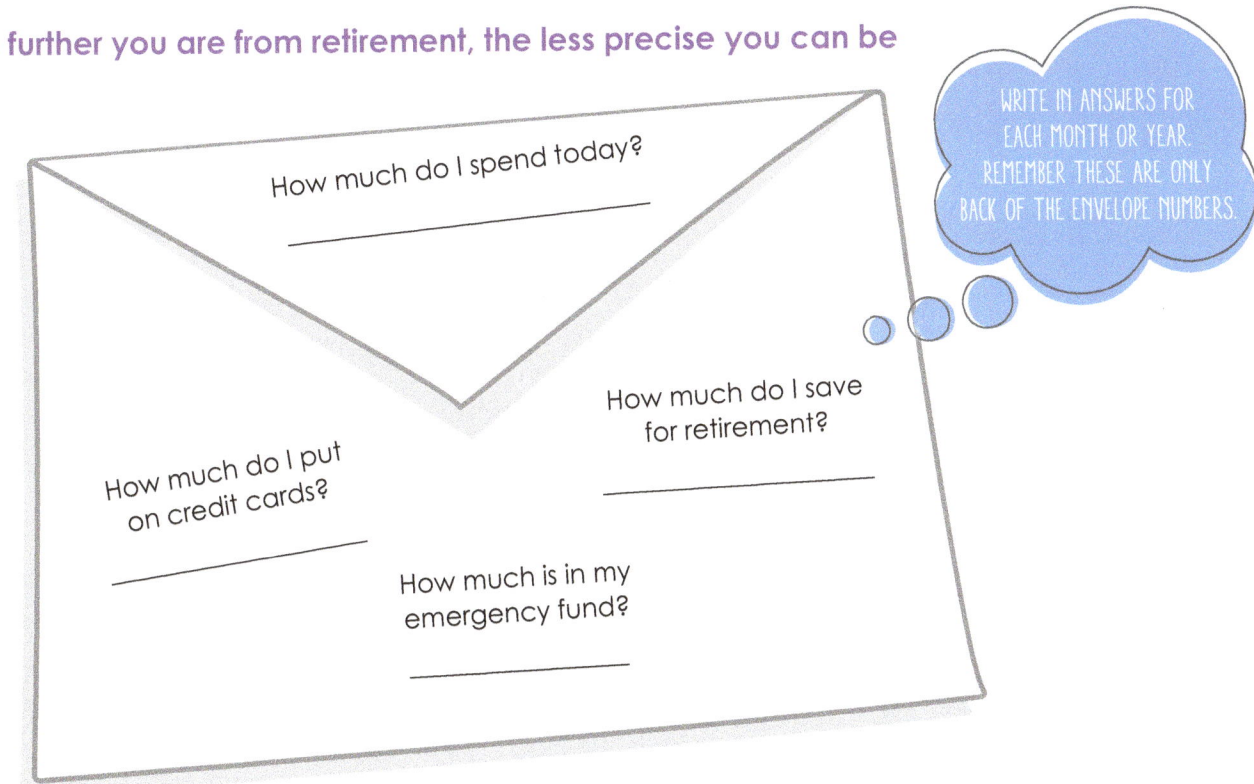

How much do I spend today?

How much do I save for retirement?

How much do I put on credit cards?

How much is in my emergency fund?

WRITE IN ANSWERS FOR EACH MONTH OR YEAR. REMEMBER THESE ARE ONLY BACK OF THE ENVELOPE NUMBERS.

The closer to retirement, the more important the details

As you think about the year you will retire, you'll need a more detailed budget. This becomes a critical tool that shows you where you'll be spending your money...and where you might cut back. Talk about these spending topics over an afternoon cup of tea and some biscuits:

- Which items are essential/must haves?
- Which categories are discretionary/nice-to-haves?
- Which costs will end during retirement?
- How much is health insurance really going to cost?
- What will my taxes look like?

Have you created a detailed budget yet? _____ yes _____ no

Make a date to lay out your baseline budget or revise your existing budget on _____

SECTION DISCUSSION 4

Separate your spending into two major categories

When creating a budget for your retirement spending, decide what is a must-have versus a nice-to-have. The must-have's are expenses you will pay for each and every month of retirement. The discretionary items can be traded off or put off in years when the value of your savings is dropping.

Essential Expenses – Must Haves	Discretionary – Nice to Haves
May be 70% - 80% of your personal spending in retirement	Some years may be more expensive than others: build in flexibility
Include costs for things that will make retirement worth doing	Items you are willing to give up in "down" years
Biggest essential expenses in retirement: taxes, health care, housing	Remember you'll have some major discretionary spending in retirement: cars, family support, travel

Your personal budget needs to account for many different situations

Think about the amount of money to reserve in each bucket – not necessarily the exact items.

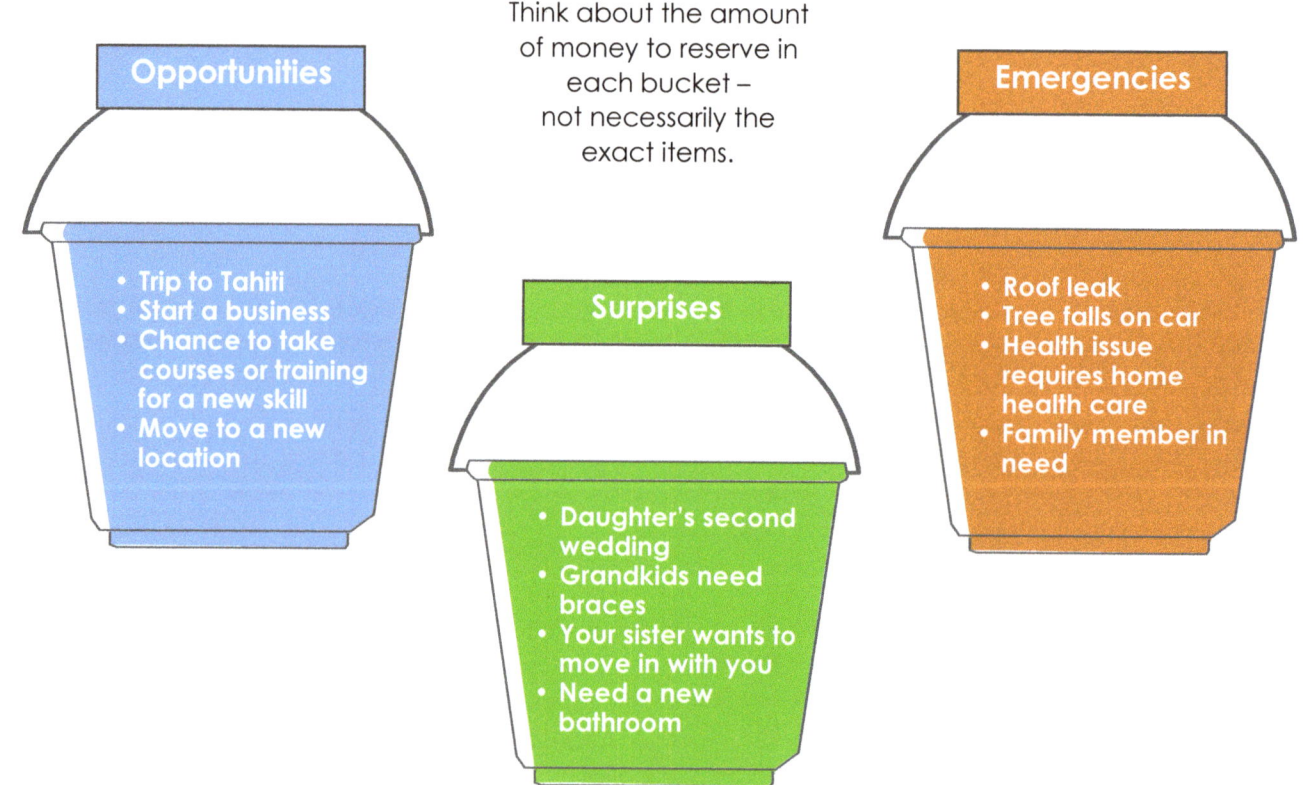

Opportunities
- Trip to Tahiti
- Start a business
- Chance to take courses or training for a new skill
- Move to a new location

Surprises
- Daughter's second wedding
- Grandkids need braces
- Your sister wants to move in with you
- Need a new bathroom

Emergencies
- Roof leak
- Tree falls on car
- Health issue requires home health care
- Family member in need

SECTION 4 DISCUSSION

Address Inflation When Planning Your Retirement Budget

- Average US inflation ranges between 2% and 3.5% since 1992, with outliers in 2021, 2022, and 2023.
- Even at low inflation, prices go up and purchasing power of investments goes down.

Declining Purchasing Power During Retirement

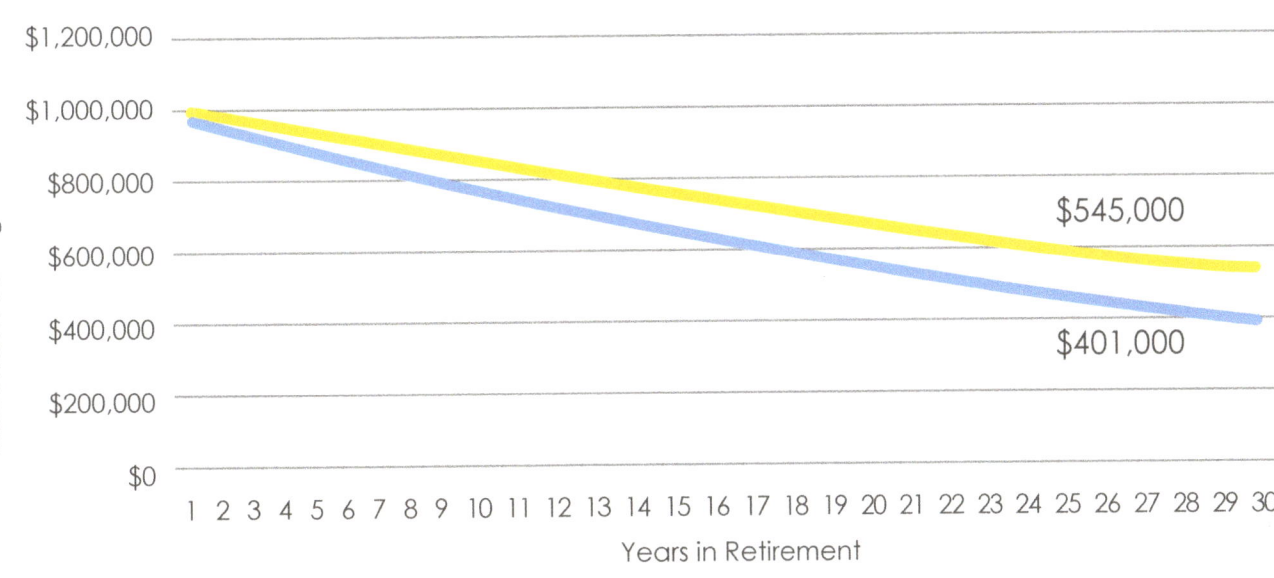

$545,000

$401,000

3% Inflation Rate   2% Inflation Rate

 **NOTE:** Plan for health care costs and insurance during retirement to rise 2x average inflation!

Plan for costs to rise over 25 years
(inflation at 2.5%)

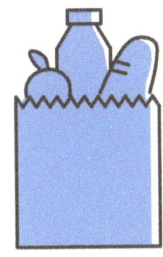

2020 = $75	2020 = $175	2020 = $37,000
2045 = $139	2045 = $325	2045 = $68,000

 ► Fill out the **"My Budget Planning Guide"** **worksheet.** How close were you to your back of the envelope estimates?

SECTION DISCUSSION 4

Understanding Medicare is more like mixing up a big bowl of salad fixin's

Health Insurance and other health costs will be significant in retirement.
There are 4 components to Medicare, plus many more costs to plan for.
Costs will be unique based on your personal health profile and situation.

Medicare Part A	Medicare Part B
Covers: Hospitalization Skilled Nursing Care Home Health Aides Hospice	**Covers:** Physicians and Health Care Workers Outpatient Services Durable Medical Equipment Limited Home Health Services
Medicare Part D	**Medigap (Supplemental) Insurance**
Covers: Prescription Drugs	**Covers:** Your share of costs, coinsurance, most deductibles in Parts A & B

SECTION 4 DISCUSSION

Another option for buying your health insurance in retirement is a Medicare Advantage (Part C) Plan with prescription drug coverage (MAPD). Monthly premiums are generally lower (even $0 for some plans) than Medigap, but you pay for services you use in-network and higher prices if you go out-of-network. You must be enrolled in Medicare Parts A and B before you can buy a MAPD.

In addition, you'll want to consider if you'll need any help paying for dental, vision, podiatry, or hearing. Some additional plans are available to help with your share of costs. And, most Medicare Advantage Plans include some cost coverage.

Bottom line: Health insurance in retirement is very different from employer group health plans. Each individual person must plan for all the component parts.

Estimate your specific healthcare costs on the attached worksheet. Use tools on Medicare.gov to research your options and costs. And, build in extra to pay for additional health care needs.

Section 4 Discussion Guide: How much will I spend each year in retirement? 34

MAKING THE TRANSITION TO RETIREMENT
SECTION 4: WORKSHEET

My Budget Planning Guide

1 Important Activities for Family and Friends: Essential Expenses (part 1)

Think about the kinds of activities that are central to how you nurture and support your family, friends, communities and connections. Spending on these activities can be a significant part of your retirement years.

These expenses are generally non-negotiable. You consider them integral and essential to your life. The amount you spend on each item can increase or decrease based on your yearly plans and how extravagant or frugal you want to be at any given time.

Make your best guess in these categories and add them up for a yearly view.

Keeping the family together activities:	$
Activities with friends:	$
Special days and events:	$
Outings with family and friends:	$
Bringing the kids/grandkids home:	$
Grandkids:	$
Supporting church, charity, community:	$
Gifts for family and close friends:	$
Hobbies, crafts, gardening, photography, etc. that are essential to your retirement:	$
Support for aging parents, relatives, special needs adult children:	$
Other:	$
Other:	$
YOUR TOTAL FOR ONE YEAR:	$

② Events for Friends and Family: Essential Expenses (part 2)

Now, think about where all the important people in your life live. Are they in your neighborhood or living well beyond your local area?

Making sure that your important family and friends get together periodically is especially important when they are scattered around the globe. And these gatherings become more meaningful as we add new generations.

Women typically plan holiday gatherings, weddings, and reunions. They create and sustain traditions that remind our families of our history.

Not only will you plan for the party, but you'll need to plan for the price tag as well.

Put in at least some broad guesses as to how much these types of annual events cost. Think about how large your budget might be for occasions such as weddings and large family reunions.

Party Food / Party Fare / Decorations:	$
Spring Holidays:	$
Summer Holidays:	$
Fall Holidays:	$
Winter Holidays:	$
Birthdays, Anniversaries, Special Days:	$
Gifts:	$
Transportation you pay for (airplane or train tickets, rental cars, gas, etc.):	$
New outfits / accessories / shoes for special events:	$
Other:	$
Other:	$
Other:	$
Other:	$
YOUR TOTAL FOR ONE YEAR:	$

Weddings – your daughter's, your son's, other family and friends:	$ (one-time expense)
Reunions – high school, college, family, etc.:	$ (periodic expense)
Other one-time expense:	$
Other one-time expense:	$

3 Cost of Running your Household: Essential Expenses (part 3)

You'll want to keep your home and household running smoothly after your paycheck stops. Knowing what all of the basics are and how much it costs to "keep the lights on" is critical to every retirement plan.

The items listed in this section are generally considered essential expenses and will need to be paid for every month as long as you or your spouse/partner is alive. This is your "must have to live" list.

Use your checkbook and credit card statements to get a realistic set of numbers for what it takes you to maintain your household.

If any of the expenses will be eliminated, make a note of the year they will be completed.

Keep in mind that for the most part, costs to run your house will increase each year.

Groceries:	$
Dining out (is this essential for you?):	$
Home – mortgage / rent:	$
Maintenance, fees & upkeep:	$
Health Insurance:	$
Medicare:	$
Supplemental Insurance:	$
Dental, Vision, Hearing:	$
Prescriptions:	$
Other Out of Pocket:	$
Car payments:	$
Maintenance & gas:	$
Public Transportation:	$
Utilities (electric, cable, fuel, water, etc.):	$
Phones, cell phones:	$
Technology – computer, providers, security, staying connected:	$
Insurance Payments (auto, homeowners, renter's, life, disability, etc.):	$
Taxes (income, auto, property, etc.):	$
Pets:	$
Other:	$
Other:	$
Other:	$
YOUR TOTAL FOR ONE YEAR:	$

4 Household Discretionary/ Flexible Expenses (part 4)

There are lots of extras that might be part of your retirement years. It's fun to plan for these items, but it's important to recognize that you might have to compromise on some of them some of the time.

These should be activities and items you can scale back on or give up in years where your savings may be lower than ideal. Spending on these items needs to be flexible.

Think of Items that you would be willing to trade off from time to time but not ones that take away from the very reasons you enjoy your retirement.

You may also want to provide a financial legacy to your children or grandchildren. Think about how much you might want to gift on an annual basis or as a one-time legacy.

Vacations:	$
Extended travel plans:	$
General Entertainment:	$
Dining out frequently:	$
Movies, Shows, Events:	$
Sports:	$
Club Memberships:	$
Extensive hobbies – materials, equipment, travel, etc.:	$
Gifting assets to children (annual amount):	$
Gifting assets / college savings for grandchildren (annual estimates):	$
Other:	$
Other:	$
Other:	$
Other:	$
Other:	$
Other:	$
YOUR TOTAL FOR ONE YEAR:	$

New car purchase – every _____ years:	$
Optional "nice to have" home improvements:	$
Home modifications for aging in place:	$
Legacy assets to children (total $):	$
Legacy assets to grandchildren (total $):	$

How much will Medicare and other health coverage cost?

Costs for your health insurance, prescription drugs, and other needs may be a significant part of your budget in retirement. Each individual will have his or her own set of costs. Try your hand at laying out your own costs for coverage. Start with the Medicare components, then add in other estimates.

Start with the current year, then estimate costs for additional years using an inflation rate of 5% for premiums and services, and 7% for the cost of drugs (capped at $2,000/year).

Medicare Component	Estimated Cost (Current Year)	Estimated Cost Year ____	Estimated Cost Year ____	Estimated Cost Year ____
Medicare Part A premium (usually $0)				
Medicare Part B base premium				
Medicare Part B deductible				
Part B IRMAA				
Medigap or MAPD copays				
Part D premium				
Part D IRMAA				
Cost of Rx #1 – generic				
Cost of Rx #2 – specialty				
TOTAL COSTS per person				

Other Health Costs expected in retirement	Estimated Cost (Current Year)	Estimated Cost Year ____	Estimated Cost Year ____	Estimated Cost Year ____
Dental – basic				
Dental – major				
Vision – exams				
Vision – glasses, contacts				
Hearing – exams				
Hearing aids				
Podiatry services, non-covered				
OTC - drugs				
OTC - other				
TOTAL COSTS per person				

Planning with a spouse or partner?

Health insurance is individually selected and priced in retirement. If planning with a spouse or partner, they also need to research their costs and options.

While some insurers offer discounts if both spouses use their products, there is no need for both individuals to use the same insurer. Make sure to read the fine print. Discounts are often available only in the first year or two!

Medicare Component	Estimated Cost (Current Year)	Estimated Cost Year _____	Estimated Cost Year _____	Estimated Cost Year _____
Medicare Part A premium (usually $0)				
Medicare Part B base premium				
Medicare Part B deductible				
Part B IRMAA				
Medigap or MAPD copays				
Part D premium				
Part D IRMAA				
Cost of Rx #1 – generic				
Cost of Rx #2 – specialty				
TOTAL COSTS per person				

Other Health Costs expected in retirement	Estimated Cost (Current Year)	Estimated Cost Year _____	Estimated Cost Year _____	Estimated Cost Year _____
Dental – basic				
Dental – major				
Vision – exams				
Vision – glasses, contacts				
Hearing – exams				
Hearing aids				
Podiatry services, non-covered				
OTC - drugs				
OTC - other				
TOTAL COSTS per person				

Build a Retirement Income "Paycheck" with Your Ingredients

Now that you've seen up close how much you really do spend on everything from groceries to gifts and grandkids, you're aware that retirement is not so cheap. But fear not! You've clipped coupons, scrimped, and saved for decades for just this time in your life.

In this section of the guidebook, you'll pull together all your financial resources so you can see how you'll create a reliable stream of monthly income when your employer paycheck stops. It's like pulling together all the ingredients to make a lasagna.

Have a seat at your kitchen table and talk about your money. You'll want to figure out how you'll make it work to pay for the basics and the extras when your paycheck stops.

Think about the amount of income your personal savings need to produce in retirement. Focus on three key areas. They are your overall financial goals in retirement:

1 Create enough cash every month to pay all your bills and meet your spending needs – as long as you live

2 Build in flexibility to cover unknown expenses – opportunities, surprises, and emergencies

3 Invest so your assets deliver more dollars over time as inflation erodes purchasing power

What sources of income will you have to create your paycheck throughout retirement? These are the financial ingredients to make your "lasagna."

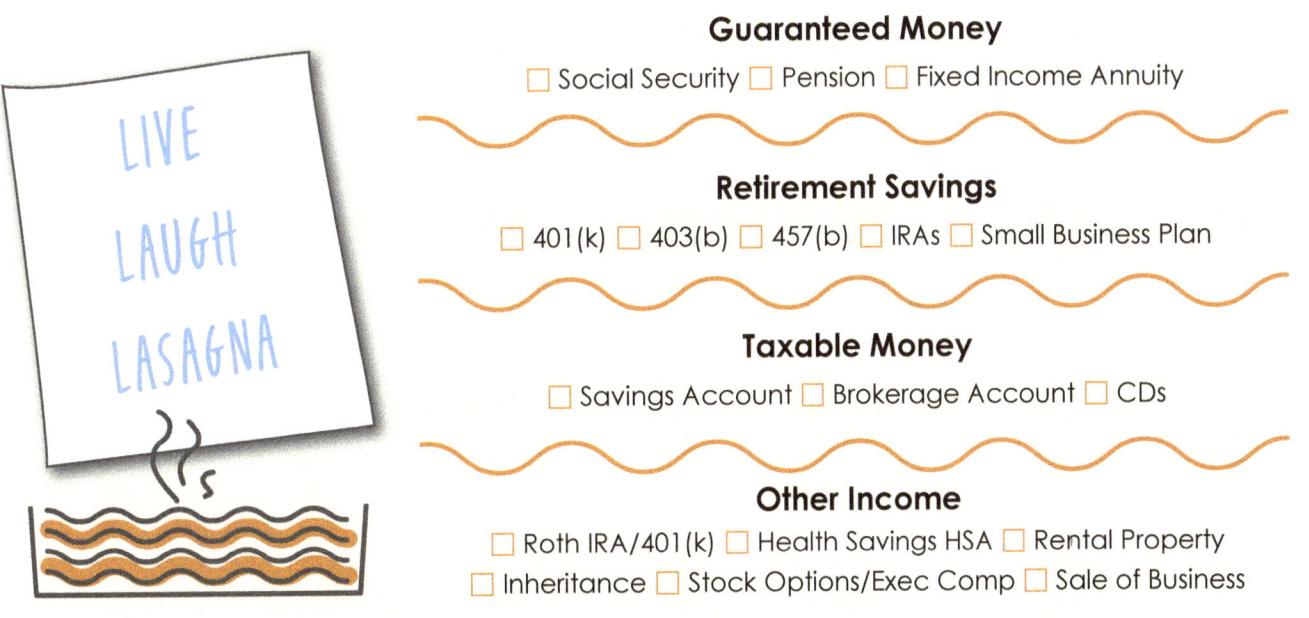

Guaranteed Money
☐ Social Security ☐ Pension ☐ Fixed Income Annuity

Retirement Savings
☐ 401(k) ☐ 403(b) ☐ 457(b) ☐ IRAs ☐ Small Business Plan

Taxable Money
☐ Savings Account ☐ Brokerage Account ☐ CDs

Other Income
☐ Roth IRA/401(k) ☐ Health Savings HSA ☐ Rental Property
☐ Inheritance ☐ Stock Options/Exec Comp ☐ Sale of Business

SECTION 5 DISCUSSION

Will you consider working in retirement? In what capacity?

☐ Yes ☐ No ☐ Would consider for good opportunity

@ Current Employer	@ New Employer	Start a Small Biz
☐ Part-time ☐ Phased ☐ Consulting	☐ Part-time ☐ Phased ☐ Consulting	☐ Consulting ☐ Convert hobby to biz ☐ Hang own shingle ☐ Start up dream idea
Starting: Ending:	Starting: Ending:	Starting: Ending:

How much income can you squeeze from each orange in your grocery bag?

Your job may have come with an important retirement benefit: a pension. If so, that monthly payment will become a key piece of your retirement paycheck.

You may also consider purchasing an annuity for a guaranteed stream of income. Many retirees find a fixed income annuity stretches out their savings if they live a long time.

If either source is available to you, that is good news! You'll want to squeeze every dollar from these sources. Carefully consider payment options when you are alive AND if you should die before your spouse or partner.

Pensions & Fixed Income Annuities: Monthly amounts depend on key choices

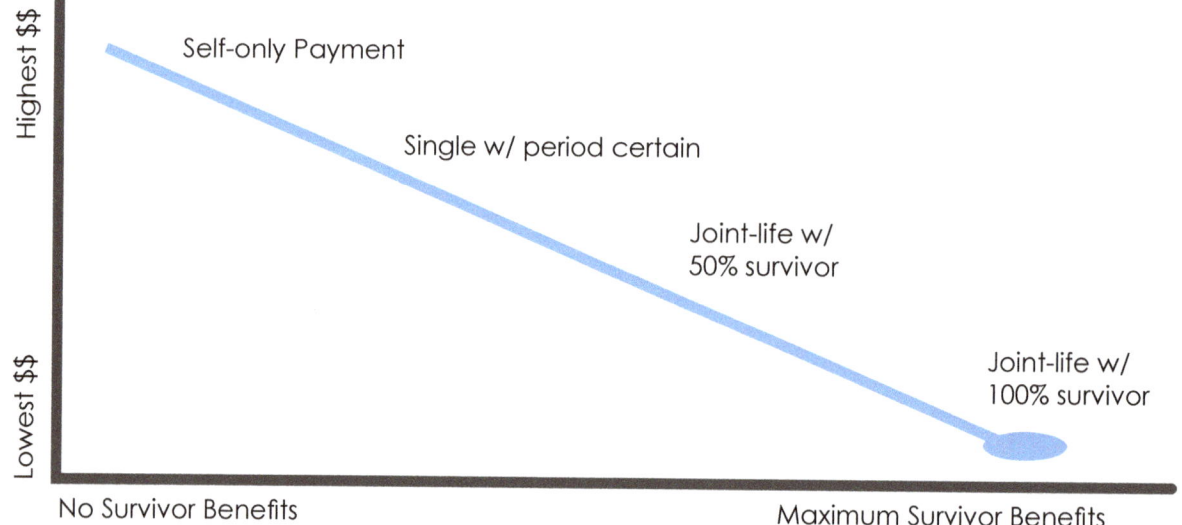

SECTION 5 DISCUSSION

Social Security is the foundation to your retirement income plan

Like that first layer of lasagna, your first layer of income in retirement needs to be sturdy to hold up the rest of the layers. Otherwise, they collapse.

Social Security is your first layer. And may be your most important ingredient. The decision you make about when to claim is one of the single most important financial decisions of your entire next 30 years. You are faced with many choices about Social Security in your early 60s. That decision impacts how secure your income will be in your 80s and 90s and even if you reach 100!

For much more complete information about Social Security, how it works, how your benefit is calculated, and how to claim if you are married, divorced, widowed, or single, get a copy of my book. Available on Amazon.com and BarnesandNoble.com

Social Security:
Get more if you claim later

24% MORE

Optimal Income at FRA

30% LESS

Secret ingredients to making the best Social Security claiming decision for you

- While the early claiming "gate" opens at age 62, this is rarely the best time to claim. You'll lock in a permanent reduction in monthly income up to 30%.
- Your optimal benefit is calculated at your Full Retirement Age (FRA). It's between 66 and 67.
- There are some situations where you might benefit by waiting until age 70 to claim your maximum benefit. You'll get an 8% per year delayed "bonus."
- If you are the higher-earning spouse, your claiming decision may leave your spouse with less income. Lower-earning surviving spouses receive your benefit amount, but lose their own.
- If you are divorced and unmarried when you claim, you may be eligible to claim on your ex. There are lots of rules, but if it works out, you may get more Social Security than you know.
- When you are ready to claim, find your checklist on BoomerRetirementBriefs.com. Download your free copy so you won't miss a step.

SECTION 5
DISCUSSION

POP QUIZ

Test your Knowledge:
Take the Social Security quiz on the following page.
See how much you really know!

▶ **Action Step:** *Set up your my Social Security Account at SSA.gov and download your current statement and full earnings history.*

**Social Security is a special kind of income source in retirement.
As important as chocolate or wine.
But, how much do you really know?**

Take a few minutes to answer the following questions – Then check the post on
Boomer Retirement Briefs to see how to see how many you correctly answered.
(https://boomerretirementbriefs.com/social-security-answers/)

Question	Your Answer	Actual Answer
What is your Full Retirement Age (FRA)?	a. 60 b. 62 c. 65 d. It depends	
How many years of income does Social Security use to calculate your benefit?	a. Highest 5 b. Last 3 c. Highest 35 d. Last 10	
How many "credits" do you need to earn to be independently eligible for Social Security?	a. 40 b. 30 c. 20 d. 10	
For average wage-earners, how much income does Social Security typically replace?	a. 25% b. 40% c. 70% d. 90%	
What is the maximum benefit amount paid to those who reach FRA in 2021?	a. $2,500 b. $3,148 c. $5,723 d. $8,644	
At what age do you receive your maximum Social Security payment?	a. Your FRA b. 65 c. 70 d. 75	
True or False? Your Social Security payment will be reduced once you start Medicare Part B?	a. True b. False	
True or False? If you don't have your own work record, or it is not sufficient, you can't get any Social Security benefits?	a. True b. False	
Divorced individuals may be able to claim on their ex-spouse. How much might they receive of their ex's benefit amount?	a. Up to 25% b. Up to 50% c. Up to 75% d. Up to 90%	
True or False? If you become a surviving spouse, you will keep your own benefit, plus receive 50% of your deceased spouse's benefit?	a. True b. False	

Use your own investments and savings to create the balance of your retirement paycheck

Your Portfolio: Managing withdrawal rates is key to creating sustainable income and providing long-range growth opportunities

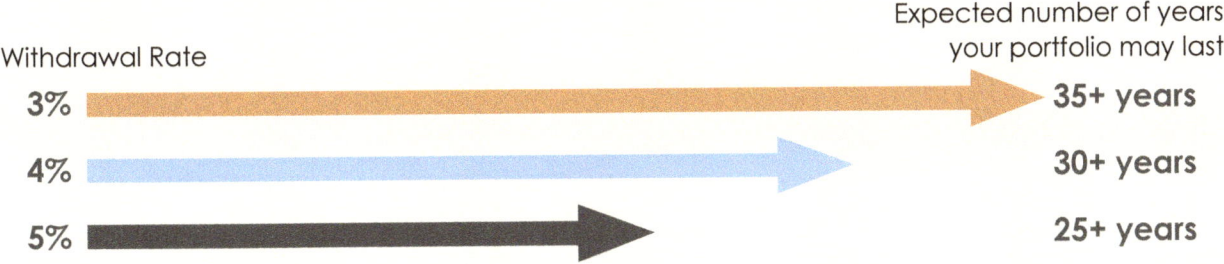

Withdrawal Rate

Expected number of years your portfolio may last

3% → 35+ years

4% → 30+ years

5% → 25+ years

Plan to withdraw lower percentages of your savings early in retirement when you have a longer horizon

Amount Saved	1st Year Withdrawal @ 4% Monthly Amount	1st Year Withdrawal @ 4% Yearly Amount
$250,000	$833	$10,000
$500,000	$1,667	$20,000
$1,000,000	$3,333	$40,000

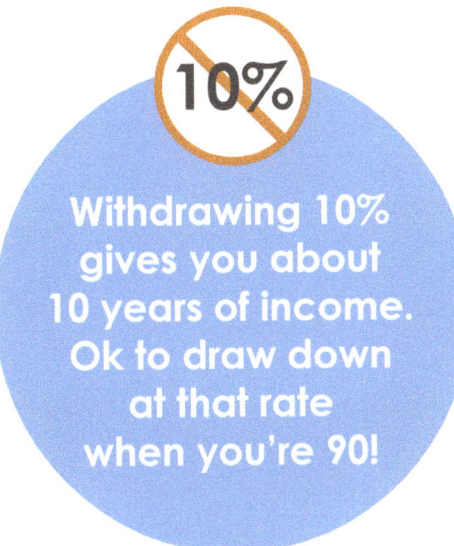

10%

Withdrawing 10% gives you about 10 years of income. Ok to draw down at that rate when you're 90!

RMDs: All tax-deferred retirement savings accounts must begin Required Minimum Distributions when you reach age 72 (if born in 1950), 73 (if born between 1951-1959), or 75 (if born 1960 or later), except plans at your current employer, if you are still working.

- Your income tax obligation has been deferred during your accumulation years. Now, it's time to pay up.
- RMDs are assessed at your ordinary income tax rate in the year you withdraw funds.
- IRS rules determine the minimum you must withdraw and include in your taxable income each year.
- If you do not withdraw at least the minimum every year, you may be assessed a **25%** tax penalty!

Age	Distribution Period (yrs)	% Withdrawal
*72	27.4	3.65%
*73	26.5	3.77%
74	25.5	3.92%
*75	24.6	4.07%
76	23.7	4.22%
77	22.9	4.37%
78	22	4.55%
79	21.1	4.74%
80	20.2	4.95%
81	19.4	5.15%
82	18.5	5.41%
83	17.7	5.65%
84	16.8	5.95%
85	16	6.25%
86	15.2	6.58%
87	14.4	6.94%
88	13.7	7.30%
89	12.9	7.75%
90	12.2	8.20%
91	11.5	8.70%

Age	Distribution Period (yrs)	% Withdrawal
92	10.8	9.26%
93	10.1	9.90%
94	9.5	10.53%
95	8.9	11.24%
96	8.4	11.90%
97	7.8	12.82%
98	6.8	13.70%
99	7.3	14.71%
100	6.4	15.63%
101	6	16.67%
102	5.6	17.86%
103	5.2	19.23%
104	4.9	20.41%
105	4.6	21.74%
106	4.3	23.26%
107	4.1	24.39%
108	3.9	25.64%
109	3.7	27.03%
110	3.5	28.57%

RMDs are due on these accounts every year.

Which accounts do you own?

- ☐ Traditional IRA
- ☐ Rollover IRA
- ☐ 401(k)
- ☐ 403(b)
- ☐ 457(b)
- ☐ SEP IRA
- ☐ SIMPLE IRA
- ☐ Profit Sharing plans
- ☐ Other defined contribution plans

- RMDs are NOT due on your personal Roth IRAs, but are required if you inherit a Roth IRA

- Inherited IRAs have different RMD rules

- Different rules apply if using RMDs for qualified charitable giving

- This table can be used for many individuals*

GET COOKIN'! ▶ *Find all your tax-deferred account balances and list them in the Section 5 worksheet.*

*Unmarried Owners, Married Owners whose spouses aren't more than 10 years younger, and Married Owners whose spouses aren't the sole beneficiaries of their IRAs use this table. Find all current IRS RMD tables on the Federal Register website or IRS Publication 590-B.

MAKING THE TRANSITION TO RETIREMENT
SECTION 5: WORKSHEET

Search Your Pantry for your Tax-Deferred Accounts

Where are your tax-deferred accounts? And how many do you have?

You may have more retirement savings accounts than you think. After 40+ years working, it's not uncommon to have 4-to-10 different IRAs and other employer plans, pensions, annuities, and the like.

Take some time to find all your accounts and note which financial institution holds each account.

Keep in mind, every tax-deferred account you own will have a required minimum distribution beginning the year you reach 72, 73 or 75. If you are still working, then you may delay the RMD on that employer's plan until you retire. (There are different rules if you are the business owner.) Check the details with your tax professional.

Type of Tax-Deferred Account	Approximate Value	Financial Institution
Traditional IRA	$	
Rollover IRA	$	
401(k)	$	
403(b)	$	
457(b)	$	
SEP IRA	$	
SIMPLE IRA	$	
Annuities	$	
Other Plans	$	
NQDC	$	

▶ **Action Step:** _Follow IRS rules_ to calculate an estimate of your RMDs.
(https://www.irs.gov/retirement-plans/plan-participant-employee/required-minimum-distribution-worksheets)

Planning with a spouse or partner?

Keep in mind that all retirement accounts are considered "individual" accounts. There is only one owner per account. If you're planning for retirement with your spouse or partner, make sure to also locate all their accounts and note where they are housed as well.

Type of Tax-Deferred Account	Approximate Value	Financial Institution
Traditional IRA	$	
Rollover IRA	$	
401(k)	$	
403(b)	$	
457(b)	$	
SEP IRA	$	
SIMPLE IRA	$	
Annuities	$	
Other Plans	$	
NQDC	$	

More Income Information For You

Look in your cupboards for additional accounts and resources available to build your retirement paycheck

While most folks typically think of 401(k)s, 403(b)s and IRAs as their main sources of income for retirement, you may well have other sources to work with. Consider Social Security, pensions, taxable and tax-free accounts, and future income sources.

What are your Social Security options?

Create your account and download your current Social Security statement at SSA.gov.

Your Full Retirement Age (FRA) is _____ and you reach it on _____ (mo.) _____ (yr.)

Estimated monthly amount if you file at your FRA = $ _____

If you claim early, what age will you choose? _____ How much will you receive? $ _____

How much less than your FRA amount? $ _____

If you claim after FRA, what age will you be? _____ How much will you receive? $ _____

How much more than your FRA amount? $ _____

If you are married and have the higher benefit amount, how much will your spouse receive if you die first? $ _____

Do you have a pension?

Check with your pension administrator to confirm the rules for starting your pension, the options for receiving payments, and the amounts you'll be paid over a single life or over two lives.

Pension payments can begin as early as _____ (date)

Amount if paid on a single life = $ _____

Amount if paid over joint lives = $ _____

Amount my spouse or beneficiary would receive if I am first to die = $ _____

Is a lump-sum option available? $ _____

If so, is it in my best interest to consider this option? _____

If this is a state or public pension, have I adjusted any Social Security benefits due to the pension? _____

Am I subject to the Windfall Elimination Provision (WEP) or Government Pension Offset (GPO)? _____

What other resources do you have to tap for income?

Use these tables to organize your full inventory of every type of asset and account you have that might be used to create some of your retirement income. Each asset may not yet be available (sale of your house, for example), but it's important to keep track of what your options may be.

Other Accounts	Approximate Value	Financial Institution
Savings Account	$	
Brokerage Account	$	
CDs	$	
Roth IRA	$	
Roth 401(k)	$	
Health Savings Account (HSA)	$	
Stock Options	$	
Executive Compensation	$	
Rental Property	$	
Other	$	
Other	$	

Future Resources that May Become Available	Approximate Value	Notes
Sale of Property	$	
Sale of Primary Residence	$	
Sale of Business	$	
Life Insurance	$	
Inheritance	$	
Other	$	
Other	$	

For Your Spouse/Partner

If you are planning with another person, make sure to account for all of their assets and income sources as well.

What are your Social Security options?

Create your account and download your current Social Security statement at SSA.gov.

Your Full Retirement Age (FRA) is _____ and you reach it on _____ (mo.) _____ (yr.)

Estimated monthly amount if you file at your FRA = $ _____

If you claim early, what age will you choose? _____ How much will you receive? $ _____

How much less than your FRA amount? $ _____

If you claim after FRA, what age will you be? _____ How much will you receive? $ _____

How much more than your FRA amount? $ _____

If you are married and have the higher benefit amount,
how much will your spouse receive if you die first? $ _____

Do you have a pension?

Check with your pension administrator to confirm the rules for starting your pension, the options for receiving payments, and the amounts you'll be paid over a single life or over two lives.

Pension payments can begin as early as _____ (date)

Amount if paid on a single life = $ _____

Amount if paid over joint lives = $ _____

Amount my spouse or beneficiary would receive if I am first to die = $ _____

Is a lump-sum option available? $ _____

If so, is it in my best interest to consider this option? _____

If this is a state or public pension, have I adjusted any Social Security benefits due to the pension? _____

Am I subject to the Windfall Elimination Provision (WEP) or Government Pension Offset (GPO)? _____

Other resources your spouse/partner has to tap for income?

Other Accounts	Approximate Value	Financial Institution
Savings Account	$	
Brokerage Account	$	
CDs	$	
Roth IRA	$	
Roth 401(k)	$	
Health Savings Account (HSA)	$	
Stock Options	$	
Executive Compensation	$	
Rental Property	$	
Other	$	
Other	$	

Future Resources that May Become Available	Approximate Value	Notes
Sale of Property	$	
Sale of Primary Residence	$	
Sale of Business	$	
Life Insurance	$	
Inheritance	$	
Other	$	
Other	$	

SECTION 6: DISCUSSION GUIDE

Estate Planning or Family Legacy Planning? You need both.

Pour a cup of coffee or glass of wine. Sit down at your kitchen table to discuss some of the most important decisions you'll make for you and for your family.

- **Estate planning** is a formal, legal, process for determining your financial, tax, and health-related decisions and documenting those decisions. You'll need your estate plan in place to handle incapacity and health issues AND how to disburse your assets upon death.

- **Legacy planning** goes beyond estate planning. It is how you define and express what wealth means to your family (even if it's not a million dollars!). It also gives you the opportunity to document what you want your heirs to know and remember about your journey. A legacy plan is a more informal way to ensure your core values, family heritage, and "treasures" are passed on to future generations. It's still a written document, but separate from the legal estate planning documents.

What's in Your Cupboard?

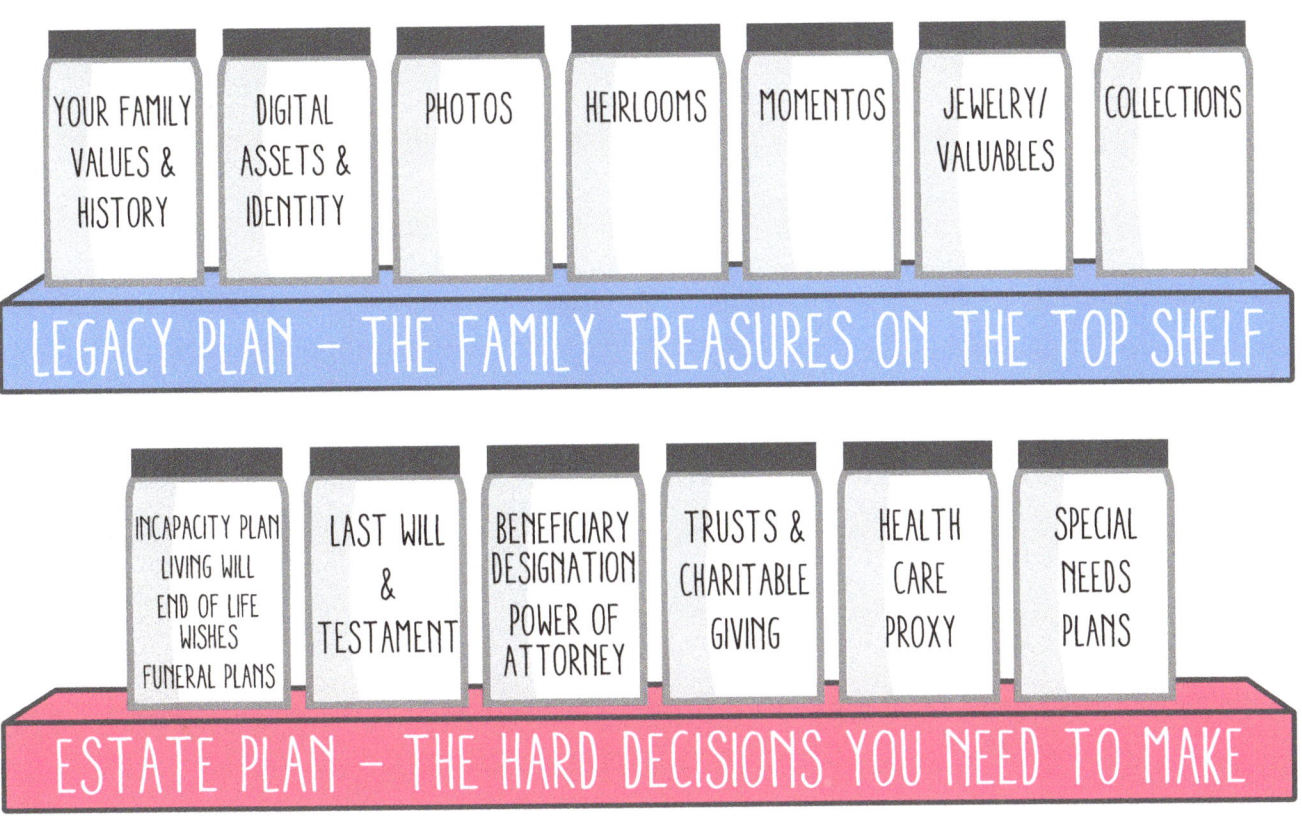

4 Major considerations when planning your estate and legacy

Who will take care of you?

_____

_____

_____

Who will get your assets and when?

_____

_____

_____

How will you preserve your family values and treasures?

_____

_____

_____

How do you ensure your wishes will be followed?

_____

_____

_____

The decisions you make for your health care and end of life are critical to document, clarify, and own.

 Action Steps:

1. *Review your estate plan and schedule an update with your attorney if it's out of date.*
2. *Devise a system for where your family legacy items will go and create a document.*

SECTION 6 DISCUSSION

More considerations when planning your estate and legacy. Grab a pen and paper and a few cookies to get started!

Gifting vs. Inheriting
- Can you afford to give limited amounts of cash to your heirs before you die?
- Gifting limits are set by the IRS and change periodically. In 2023, the limit is $17,000 per person. Check for changes to the limit each year.
- Younger generations often value the cash during their building years.

Plans for your pets
- It's critical you name the person who will take in your pet(s) when you die. Confirm that they are still willing to take care of your pet when necessary.
- Also plan for your pet(s) if you are in the hospital or need nursing care. Or if you become incapacitated or unable to care for them.
- Set aside sufficient funds to cover 2 – 3 months of care for your pet(s). Document information about your vet and any medical needs for your pet.

Digital Accounts & Passwords
- Do you have a "little black book" of all your online accounts and passwords? Everything from Amazon to Zappos should be recorded for your spouse/partner and executor to have ready access to.
- If using an online digital record keeper, make sure someone has access into your computer or phone!
- Update your passwords and record book annually.

Online photos and smart phone assets
- Whichever online photo storage you use (Dropbox, iCloud, Google, etc.) needs a password. Make sure the people you want to access your treasured photos have your detailed information and password.
- Work on organizing your digital photos for family legacy purposes.

What else do you need to add to your legacy recipe box?

RECIPES

_____

_____

_____

_____

_____

_____

_____

Generational Wealth Transfer

Preparing your assets for transfer helps retain family wealth or provide a charity with maximum value. Important steps to take involve properly documenting your current assets and ensuring your property will avoid probate where possible.

Certain property types avoid probate when properly documented

By Contract	By Law	By Trust
Beneficiaries are named and assets pass without probate Includes: IRAs, employer retirement plans, life insurance, annuities, Transfers on Death accounts (TODs) and Payable on Death accounts (PODs)	Survivors are entitled to probate-free transfer of property Includes: primary home, properly-titled JTWROS (joint tenant with rights of survivorship), Tenants by Entirety	Beneficiaries are allowed to inherit assets via transfer without probate Includes: assets transferred to living trusts before grantor's death

All other assets that pass through a will must go through probate. State laws govern the probate process. Make sure to update your estate plan if you move to a different state during retirement.

Establish a team of experts to support your wishes

SURROUND YOURSELF WITH GOOD PEOPLE
AND EAT COOKIES!

Your house may be your most important wealth transfer asset

Q: Will you consider selling your house or other family property (cabin, farm, etc.)? If so, what will you do with the proceeds while you are living? After you die?

- Consider your personal housing needs first. You need somewhere to live!
- Use housing wealth to support your retirement when needed. In many cases, your home may be your biggest asset. There are different options you might use:
    > Capital gains from sale of your home
    > HELOC (Home Equity Line of Credit)
    > HECM (Home Equity Conversion Mortgage)
    > Reverse mortgage
- Properly title your house if using a real estate trust as the owner

 **Spend some time thoughtfully filling out the "Addressing the time when you won't be here" worksheet.**

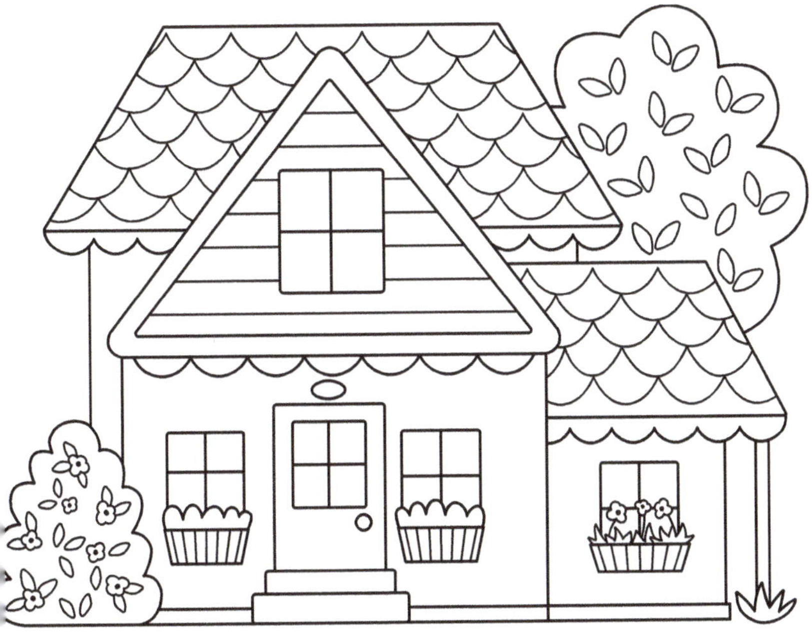

MAKING THE TRANSITION TO RETIREMENT
SECTION 6: WORKSHEET

Addressing the time when you won't be here

For You ...

The amazing dinner you made is finished. Dessert was delicious. Dishes are done. It's important to take your final bow with everything in the kitchen in its right place.

But how to get started with such sensitive topics? I'm not ready to think about getting that old!

But, it is time. And, these conversations, along with the appropriate documents, are one of the most important gifts we ever leave for our family.

4 Big Steps to Take

1 **Identify what you already have in place or schedule time to create your baseline legal documents**

☐ My latest estate plan was completed and signed on_____

☐ My executor is _____

☐ Information about my estate plan is located_____

☐ My current legacy plan is written as of _____

☐ Information about my legacy plan is located_____

2 **Ensure you have your properly named beneficiaries and TODs/PODs on every financial account**

Much of your personal wealth can pass directly to your heirs, but only if you have the proper paperwork in place. Check all your accounts for current (and living) beneficiaries.

I have checked the beneficiaries on every:

☐ IRA (Traditional, Roth, SEP, SIMPLE)

☐ 401(k), 403(b), 457(b) and any other employer plan

☐ Pension plan

☐ Annuities

☐ Life Insurance

☐ Deferred Compensation plans

☐ Health Savings Account (HSA)

☐ Other _____

I have named my TOD/POD on every one of my:

☐ Checking, Savings, CD accounts (POD)

☐ Brokerage Accounts (TOD)

☐ Individual Stocks, Bonds (TOD)

☐ Other Investments (TOD)

☐ Other _____

☐ Other _____

☐ Other _____

3   Consider a gifting strategy

It might be time to mix up a new recipe for your investments and assets.
You do not have to wait until you are gone to begin gifting some of your wealth
to younger generations or those who could benefit from your generosity today.

☐ Do I want to start reducing my taxable estate and benefit my children or grandchildren?

☐ Should I consider a Net Unrealized Appreciation strategy for my company stock?

☐ Can I help a favorite charity sooner than I expected by directing my RMD to them?

☐ Will a Donor Advised Fund be a way to support my charitable contributions?

☐ Have I explored how different trusts work and the pros and cons of using them as an estate tool
for my family and goals?

☐ Which attorney should I meet with to discuss?

☐ What other resources can be helpful as I sort through my options?

4   Plan a date with your children or trusted partner

Estate and legacy plans are less helpful if you don't bring your children into the
conversation. It is important for you to share your wishes. It helps those who
will assume care for you to truly know what you want. Time to sit around the
kitchen table and talk!

TIP: HAVE SNACKS AVAILABLE. LOTS OF SNACKS ... CHOCOLATE ...

☐ Set a date for an initial discussion with my adult children or person who

will help me in my hours of need: _____

☐ Plan an agenda for the meeting

☐ Keep the first discussion short and focused on topics most important to me:

Topic #1 _____

Topic #2 _____

Topic #3 _____

☐ Prepare to show my documents to my "people" and let them know where I keep this information

☐ Bring in a moderator or lawyer if I find I am not comfortable having these discussions

☐ What other resources may be helpful as I sort through my options?

Addressing the time when you won't be here

For Your Spouse/Partner ...

If you are planning with a spouse/partner, make sure they weigh in with their own point of view. Then the two of you can coordinate the details and be sure you know what's important to each of you.

4 Big Steps to Take

1 Identify what you already have in place or schedule time to create your baseline legal documents

☐ My latest estate plan was completed and signed on_____

☐ My executor is _____

☐ Information about my estate plan is located_____

☐ My current legacy plan is written as of _____

☐ Information about my legacy plan is located _____

2 Ensure you have your properly named beneficiaries and TODs/PODs on every financial account

Much of your personal wealth can pass directly to your heirs, but only if you have the proper paperwork in place. Check all your accounts for current (and living) beneficiaries.

I have checked the beneficiaries on every one of my:

☐ IRAs (Traditional, Roth, SEP, SIMPLE)

☐ 401(k), 403(b), 457(b) and any other employer plan

☐ Pension plan

☐ Annuities

☐ Life Insurance

☐ Deferred Compensation plans

☐ Health Savings Account (HSA)

☐ Other _____

I have named my TOD/POD on every one of my:

☐ Checking, Savings, CD accounts (POD)

☐ Brokerage Accounts (TOD)

☐ Individual Stocks, Bonds (TOD)

☐ Other Investments (TOD)

☐ Other _____

☐ Other _____

☐ Other _____

3 Consider a gifting strategy

It might be time to mix up a new recipe for your investments and assets. You do not have to wait until you are gone to begin gifting some of your wealth to younger generations or those who could benefit from your generosity today.

☐ Do I want to start reducing my taxable estate and benefit my children or grandchildren?

☐ Should I consider a Net Unrealized Appreciation strategy for my company stock?

☐ Can I help a favorite charity sooner than I expected by directing my RMD to them?

☐ Will a Donor Advised Fund be a way to support my charitable contributions?

☐ Have I explored how different trusts work and the pros and cons of using them as an estate tool for my family and goals?

☐ Which attorney should I meet with to discuss?

☐ What other resources can be helpful as I sort through my options?

4 Plan a date with your children or trusted partner

Estate and legacy plans are less helpful if you don't bring your children into the conversation. It is important for you to share your wishes. It helps those who will assume care for you to truly know what you want. Time to sit around the kitchen table and talk!

TIP: HAVE SNACKS AVAILABLE. LOTS OF SNACKS ... CHOCOLATE ...

☐ Set a date for an initial discussion with my adult children or person who

will help me in my hours of need: _____

☐ Plan an agenda for the meeting

☐ Keep the first discussion short and focused on topics most important to me:

Topic #1 _____

Topic #2 _____

Topic #3 _____

☐ Prepare to show my documents to my "people" and let them know where I keep this information

☐ Bring in a moderator or lawyer if I find I am not comfortable having these discussions

☐ What other resources may be helpful as I sort through my options?

Build your own Grab & Go Kit

One effective way to prepare for a medical emergency is to build a "Grab & Go" Hospital Kit just in case... Keep your papers in a gallon-sized baggie and hang on a door, keep in your car, etc.

These are the 10 critical ingredients every person needs to have at the ready. For detailed explanations and an infographic, read this blog post.
(https://boomerretirementbriefs.com/where-is-your-hospital-grab-go-kit-in-a-baggie-perhaps/)

▶ *Action Step:*

Set your date to build your kit:

☐ *I'm getting started today!*

_____

☐ *This is important, but needs to be done next weekend:*

_____

☐ *My to-do list is a little long right now, but I will schedule this for the 1st day of:*

_____

RECIPE: _Grab and Go Kit_____

INGREDIENTS

1. Basic personal information
2. Current medical information
3. Complete drug list
4. Important medical history a health care provider should know about you
5. Copy of your current health insurance card(s) – front and back of each
6. An original, signed HIPAA Release form
7. Signed healthcare proxy
8. MOLST - Medical Orders for Life-Sustaining Treatment
9. Power of attorney (POA)
10. Living will

Resources

Thinking about a time when you aren't here is never fun. There are many ways to approach estate planning and legacy planning. It's often a matter of finding the time to sit down and think about what you really want. Experts in these areas have many resources available, free of charge. One of the most comprehensive is The Conversation Project. *(https://theconversationproject.org/)*
If you're looking for a place to start, this is it. Other resources include:

LEGACY RESOURCES

Check out CultivateWhatMatters.com for ideas and resources to build your legacy.

Google "Preserve Family History" for a list of ideas.

ScanMyPhotos.com is a great resource for getting all your family photos into digital format. A life-long treasure of memories.

ESTATE PLANNING RESOURCES

Fidelity Investments has an excellent series on estate planning online. If you are also a customer, there is an estate planning tool to help you get organized.

File of Life is truly a life-saving, yet incredibly simple, communication tool that every EMT looks for when they arrive at your home. Make sure you have yours on the fridge!

PLAN A, B, + C

Planning Your Retirement Menu

Pulling together your time and money possibilities

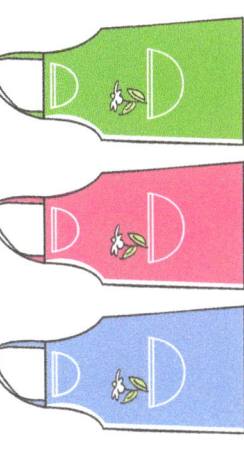

PLAN A, B, + C: Planning Your Retirement Menu

The key to your successful retirement planning is to have a clear view of where you want to go – like planning a menu for a holiday.

Now that you've had in-depth discussions at your kitchen table and spent time filling out the various worksheets in this guidebook, it's time to start "assembling your lasagna." Pull together the information you've already gathered onto the following pages where you'll:

- Identify key themes and high-level plans you want to pursue each year – from Sections 1 and 2.
- Mark your key milestones and important birthdays – from Section 3.
- Indicate approximate spending needs each year and financial resources to pay for retirement – from Sections 4 and 5.

Starting with today, map out your next 10 years. Think about key assumptions for your time and money and let your ideas take you to new places.

Start with **Plan A**. If you could make every decision for the next 10 years, what would you do? How old will you be each year? How about your spouse/partner? What are your total living expenses? And what is your household income and the value of your assets? **Plan A** becomes your ideal plan for your transition to retirement.

- Still working? Retiring early? Starting a new business?
- Moving or renovating your current house?
- Plans for traveling?
- Trying new hobbies and activities?

Take a look at the example on the following two pages for ideas and inspiration.

HOLIDAY MENU

STARTERS

MAIN

DESSERT

WHAT IF?

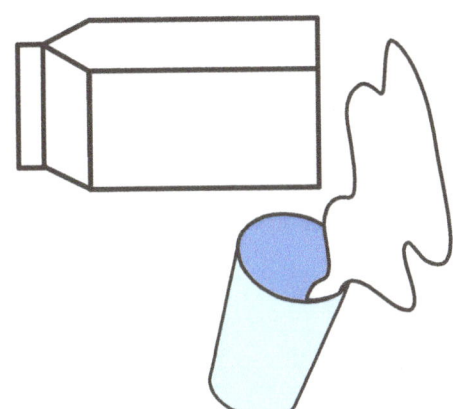

Next, consider what happens if your Plan A menu might not work.

What if the soufflé falls or the cheesecake cracks? What if you forget to add sugar to your cookies? If you spill the coffee, what happens to your time and money? Lots of mishaps can happen in the kitchen.

Use the **Plan B and Plan C** worksheets to create alternate menus. Get a closer look how you and your finances could respond to changing the menu:

Use Plan B to reflect your next 10 years if there are favorable changes.

- You decide to retire early.
- That second home you've always wanted is suddenly affordable.
- You're no longer waiting to travel – time to pack a bag and go.
- Grandbabies are arriving next year – twins!

Finally, use Plan C to consider unfavorable circumstances that could significantly change your retirement outlook.

- You or your spouse/partner lose a good job earlier than planned.
- You or someone in your close circle gets sick and needs care.
- Adult children run into hard times. They move home or require unexpected financial help.
- A natural disaster hits your home. Even with insurance, there are many additional expenses and time required to fix things up.

Map out what could change about your retirement plans and your financial picture. What pressures will be placed on your income, assets, and expenses if you find yourself in a Plan B or C situation?

Build your first set of Plan A, B, +C as your baseline. Then come back each year to revisit, revise, and revamp. Keep the ingredients you like and change the ones you don't. After all, planning for retirement is a grand experiment.

A SAMPLE CASE PLAN A: Sally's Ideal Menu

"Sally" is in her late 50s when she starts her retirement planning. She wants to make some big changes with where she lives and wants to try a 1-year relocation for fun. She needs to carefully balance her expenses with her income.

Key Assumptions:

Sally will need to: 1) Buy health insurance until Medicare at 65.
2) Claim Social Security at Full Retirement Age.
3) Keep her rental income steady.
4) Tap taxable accounts starting in year 3.

	1	2	3	4	5
	YEAR: 2020 AGE: 57 AGE:	YEAR: 2021 AGE: 58 AGE:	YEAR: 2022 AGE: 59 AGE:	YEAR: 2023 AGE: 60 AGE:	YEAR: 2024 AGE: 61 AGE::
THEME:	San Francisco Adventure	Final Year in Detroit	Blueberry Farm – yr 1	Blueberry Farm – yr 2	Blueberry Farm – yr 3
PLANS:	• Rent Condo • Move "stuff" to storage • Rent 1 year in San Francisco – dream come true!	• Move back to Condo • Freelance work • Look for hobby farm	• Rent Condo • Buy hobby farm and start new adventure • Freelance work	• Create new farm biz / products • Freelance 50%	• Grow new farm biz / products • Freelance 25% • Sell condo in Detroit
MILESTONE:				• Big birthday bash!	
ESTIMATED EXPENSES:	$100,000	$80,000	$80,000	$80,000	$80,000
ESTIMATED INCOME:	$100,000	$100,000	$50,000	$25,000	$25,000
TAXABLE ACCOUNTS:	$550,000	$550,000	$250,000	$200,000	$160,000 + $350,000
RETIREMENT INVESTMENTS:	$1,740,000	$1,800,000	$1,900,000	$2,000,000	$2,100,000
RENTAL INCOME:			$21,000	$21,000	
FARM REVENUE:					$25,000

A SAMPLE CASE PLAN A: Sally's Ideal Menu

Key Assumptions:

Sally will need to: 1) Consider tapping her IRA in year 6.

2) Ensure the farm is producing some revenue.

3) Sign up for Medicare and Social Security on time.

	6	7	8	9	10
	YEAR: 2025 AGE: 62 AGE:	YEAR: 2026 AGE: 63 AGE:	YEAR: 2027 AGE: 64 AGE:	YEAR: 2028 AGE: 65 AGE:	YEAR: 2029 AGE: 66 AGE:
THEME:	Blueberry Farm – yr 4	Blueberry Farm – yr 5	Blueberry Farm – yr 6	Blueberry Farm – yr 7	Blueberry Farm – yr 8
PLANS:	• Continue to grow new businesses / products on farm	• Continue to grow new businesses / products on farm	• Run businesses / products on farm • Sign up for Medicare in July	• Run businesses / products on farm	• Make decision about farm and retirement • Sign up for Social Security in August
MILESTONE:	Social Security opens		Medicare begins 10/1	Another birthday bash!	Social Security begins 11/1
ESTIMATED EXPENSES:	$80,000	$80,000	$80,000	$80,000	$80,000
ESTIMATED INCOME:	$0	$0	$0	$0	$0
TAXABLE ACCOUNTS:	$510,000	$490,000	$470,000	$450,000	$430,000
RETIREMENT INVESTMENTS:	$2,200,000	$2,300,000	$2,400,000	$2,500,000	$2,600,000
FARM REVENUE:	$25,000	$35,000	$35,000	$45,000	$45,000

Worksheet: Plans A, B, +C 70

PLAN A My Ideal Retirement Menu

Starting today, what do I think the next 10 years could look like? There are so many options. Do I want to keep working? Build new skills? Go back to school?

Pour a cup of coffee or tea, talk over your ideas, and pencil in your initial thoughts. You can always change them later.

Key Assumptions

_____

_____

	1	2	3	4	5
YEAR: AGE: AGE:					
THEME:					
PLANS:	• • • •	• • • •	• • • •	• • • •	• • • •
MILESTONE:					
ESTIMATED EXPENSES: $					
ESTIMATED INCOME: $					
TAXABLE ACCOUNTS: $					
RETIREMENT INVESTMENTS: $					

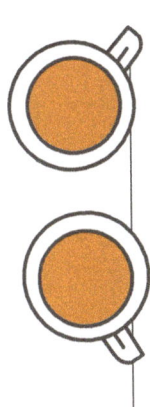

PLAN A My Ideal Retirement Menu

Key Assumptions

	6	7	8	9	10
YEAR:					
AGE: / AGE:					
THEME:					
PLANS:	• • • •	• • • •	• • • •	• • • •	• • • •
MILESTONE:					
ESTIMATED EXPENSES: $					
ESTIMATED INCOME: $					
TAXABLE ACCOUNTS: $					
RETIREMENT INVESTMENTS: $					

PLAN B An Alternate Retirement Menu

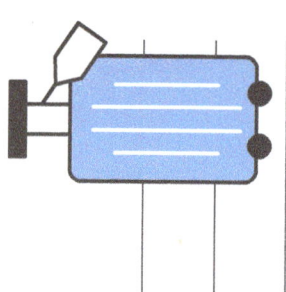

Am I ready to pack my bags and get started on some new adventure? Would I like to spend more time with my family? Do I want to keep working for a while or retire early?

Might be time for a glass of wine as you think about some of the positive alternatives to your ideal plan.

Key Assumptions

	1	**2**	**3**	**4**	**5**
YEAR: AGE: AGE:					
THEME:					
PLANS:	• • • •	• • • •	• • • •	• • • •	• • • •
MILESTONE:					
ESTIMATED EXPENSES: $					
ESTIMATED INCOME: $					
TAXABLE ACCOUNTS: $					
RETIREMENT INVESTMENTS: $					

PLAN B An Alternate Retirement Menu

Key Assumptions _____

_____

	6	**7**	**8**	**9**	**10**
YEAR:	AGE: AGE:	AGE: AGE:	AGE: AGE:	AGE: AGE:	AGE: AGE:
THEME:					
PLANS:	• • • •	• • • •	• • • •	• • • •	• • • •
MILESTONE:					
ESTIMATED EXPENSES:	$	$	$	$	$
ESTIMATED INCOME:	$	$	$	$	$
TAXABLE ACCOUNTS:	$	$	$	$	$
RETIREMENT INVESTMENTS:	$	$	$	$	$

PLAN C An Alternate Retirement Menu

Sometimes life hands you lemons. It's not always possible to make lemonade. Rather than be totally unaware of the unpleasant possibilities, better to plan for them.

Get out the ice cream and chocolate for this part of the plan. Think about the real implications if something goes wrong before you want it to. What could happen to your time, income, and assets if you lose your job or get sick?

Key Assumptions

_____

_____

1	**2**	**3**	**4**	**5**
YEAR: AGE: AGE:	YEAR: AGE: AGE:	YEAR: AGE: AGE:	YEAR: AGE: AGE:	YEAR: AGE: AGE:
THEME:	THEME:	THEME:	THEME	THEME:
PLANS: • • • •	PLANS: • • • •	PLANS: • • • •	PLANS: • • • •	PLANS: • • • •
MILESTONE:	MILESTONE:	MILESTONE:	MILESTONE:	MILESTONE:
ESTIMATED EXPENSES: $	ESTIMATED EXPENSES: $	ESTIMATED EXPENSES: $	ESTIMATED EXPENSES: $	ESTIMATED EXPENSES: $
ESTIMATED INCOME: $	ESTIMATED INCOME: $	ESTIMATED INCOME: $	ESTIMATED INCOME: $	ESTIMATED INCOME: $
TAXABLE ACCOUNTS: $	TAXABLE ACCOUNTS: $	TAXABLE ACCOUNTS: $	TAXABLE ACCOUNTS: $	TAXABLE ACCOUNTS: $
RETIREMENT INVESTMENTS: $	RETIREMENT INVESTMENTS: $	RETIREMENT INVESTMENTS: $	RETIREMENT INVESTMENTS: $	RETIREMENT INVESTMENTS: $

PLAN C An Alternate Retirement Menu

Key Assumptions

	6	7	8	9	10
YEAR:					
AGE:					
AGE:					
THEME:					
PLANS:	• • • •	• • • •	• • • •	• • • •	• • • •
MILESTONE:					
ESTIMATED EXPENSES:	$	$	$	$	$
ESTIMATED INCOME:	$	$	$	$	$
TAXABLE ACCOUNTS:	$	$	$	$	$
RETIREMENT INVESTMENTS:	$	$	$	$	$

Review, rework, reconsider your plans each year.

That way you can incorporate any changes or new decisions.

You can download a new copy of **Plan A, B, +C** on BoomerRetirementBriefs.com.

Meet the Author

Marcia Mantell is a mother, wife, daughter, sister, aunt, and now a great-aunt. She is also a Baby Boomer who embraces the journey she's been on and looks forward to a rollicking fun retirement with her husband, college sweetheart, Dan.

In 2005, she started Mantell Retirement Consulting, Inc., while raising two incredible daughters. She's spent the last 30 years talking to Baby Boomers about retirement and making 15,000 dinners for her family.

She spends a lot of time in the kitchen. This is where family and friends gather. It's where stories are told and secrets are shared. And it's where great plans for retirement get their start.

Marcia would love to hear about the retirement discussions you're having at your table. Contact her on Twitter or Threads (@MarciaMantell) or Facebook (BoomerRetirementBriefs2022).

Books and Blog by Marcia: While written for women with high hopes women will read them, they are a must-read for men. Available on Amazon and Barnes & Noble.

What's the Deal with Retirement Planning for Women?

What's the Deal with Social Security for Women?

BoomerRetirementBriefs.com is her lighthearted blog that looks at how Baby Boomers are reshaping and redefining retirement. Plus, you'll find loads of information on Social Security and Medicare.

Acknowledgments

Books don't write and design themselves, and sometimes they get off schedule. I am incredibly grateful my designer extraordinaire, Geralyn Miller, was with me every step of the way. She has a gift for making my ideas come to life on a page. I hope you enjoy every single one of the images she's created for the Marcia's Retirement Kitchen collection.

My wonderful husband, Dan Mantell, has also been with me from the beginning. He's my biggest fan and champion. If he didn't already have an important job, he would be an amazing agent for me. Thanks for testing out the Plan A, B, +C with me. It really was fun to think about! After 40-something years, I still love you best Dan.

This discussion guidebook is the result of many discussions with Baby Boomers who were looking for a place to start their retirement planning. They wanted to retire but didn't know how to begin. It can be daunting without a good recipe. My thanks go to the all the Boomers who went through early versions in PDF files. And special thanks to David and Amy Mantell and Julia Berkley and Jeffrey Cramer who helped push the content over the finish line.

Published in the USA

1st – December 2022
2nd – July 2024

ISBN 979-8-9874249-0-2